Living a Life of Purpose

Edited by
Sheree Parris Nudd

La Tour Press

Living a Life of Purpose

Copyright © 2005 by Sheree Parris Nudd

All rights reserved in all media.
ISBN 0-9755845-2-9

Published by
La Tour Press
P.O. Box 506
Brookeville, MD 20833

Visit www.DesignsforGiving.com

Printed in the United States of America. Written permission must be secured from the publisher to use or reproduce any part of this book, except for brief quotations in critical reviews or articles.

Living a Life of Purpose

Look for more gift books from
www.DesignsforGiving.com

Living a Life of Significance

Living a Life of Courage

Living a Life of Abundance

Living a Life of Purpose

Dedication

To all who are intent on living a life of purpose.

Living a Life of Purpose

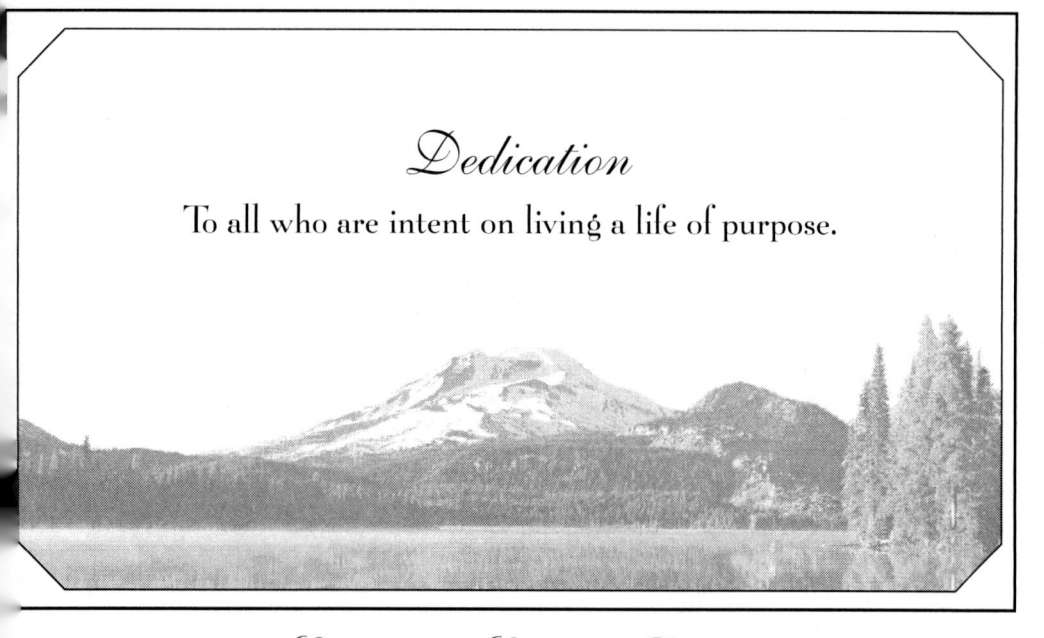

How it all started . . .

It was the mid-eighties when we first collaborated on a collection of quotations on philanthropy in booklet form. We called it "Accent on Philanthropy." A second volume later gave rise to the "Giving Is Caring Page-A-Day Calendar."

In the intervening years, more than 700,000 "Giving Is Caring" calendars have been published – spreading wise words about making a difference in the world. The "Giving Is Caring Calendar" continues today (see www.PhilanthropicGIFT.com).

Now it gives us great pleasure to present "Living a Life of Purpose" as the next volume in an ongoing series of thought-provoking gift books.

Milton Murray, FAHP   Sheree Parris Nudd, FAHP

Introduction

When we're living a life of purpose, so many things just seem to fall into place, don't they? It's as if just what's needed to live an authentic life is provided. But I prefer to believe that this is not just due to coincidence – rather, it's due to ***providence***.

Granted, a purposeful life will continue to have its difficulties. Knowing your life's direction certainly doesn't prevent all misfortune. But let me assure you that negotiating everyday challenges can be more rewarding when you're on the journey toward living a life of purpose!

Sheree

Living a Life of Purpose

More powerful than the will to win is the courage to begin.

Anonymous

Living a Life of Purpose

Our greatest need and most difficult achievement is to find meaning in our lives.

Bruno Bettelheim

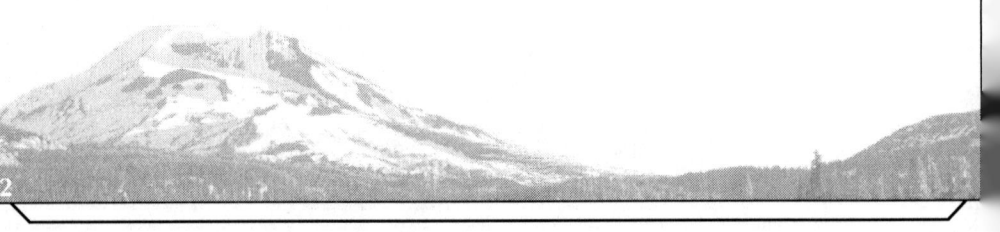

Living a Life of Purpose

The purpose of life is to matter – to count, to stand for some difference that we lived at all.

Leo Rosten

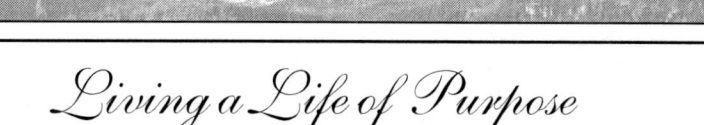

Living a Life of Purpose

I walked for miles at night along the beach, composing bad blank verse and searching endlessly for someone wonderful who would step out of the darkness and change my life. It never crossed my mind that that person could be me.

Anna Quindlen

Living a Life of Purpose

Bravery is being the only one who knows you're afraid.

Franklin P. Jones

Living a Life of Purpose

Make the most of the best and the least of the worst.

Robert Louis Stevenson

Living a Life of Purpose

Hold yourself responsible for a higher standard than anybody expects of you. Never excuse yourself.

Henry Ward Beecher

Living a Life of Purpose

What looks like a loss may be the very event which is subsequently responsible for helping to produce the major achievement of your life.

Srully D. Blotnick

Living a Life of Purpose

I attribute my success to this: I never gave or took an excuse.

Florence Nightengale

Living a Life of Purpose

> Everyone can see difficulties in opportunities, but a wise person discovers opportunities in difficulties.
>
> **Ron D. Barbaro**

Living a Life of Purpose

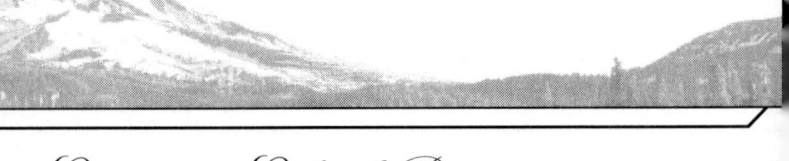

I believe we are here on planet earth to live, grow up and do what we can to make this world a better place for all people to enjoy freedom.

Rosa Parks

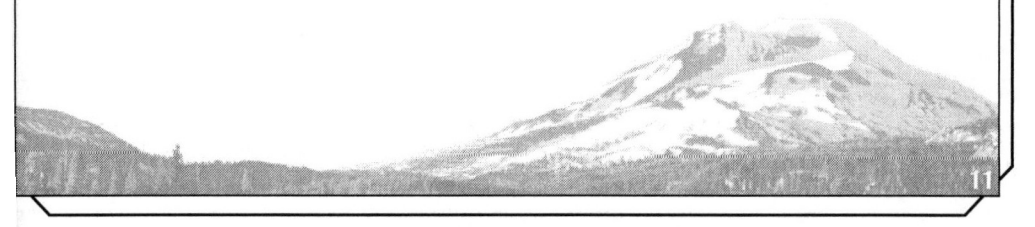

Living a Life of Purpose

Along the way of our service to others and community, we learn that a very large side benefit is an enormous sense of personal satisfaction, personal purpose and personal worth.

Brian O'Connell

Living a Life of Purpose

Giving starts with loving. Only as we are able to love others do we learn to give.

Anonymous

Living a Life of Purpose

Never think you need to apologize for asking someone to give to a worthy project...

John D. Rockefeller

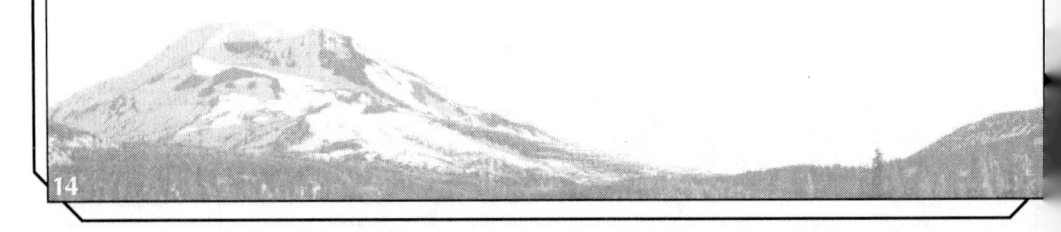

Living a Life of Purpose

More people should learn to tell their dollars where to go instead of asking them where they went.

Roger Babson

Living a Life of Purpose

It is better to give than to lend, and it costs about the same.

Sir Philip Gibbs

Living a Life of Purpose

Once you have money, you can quite truthfully affirm that money isn't everything.

Louis Kronenberger

Living a Life of Purpose

We act as though comfort and luxury were the chief requirements of life, when all that we need to make us really happy is something to be enthusiastic about.

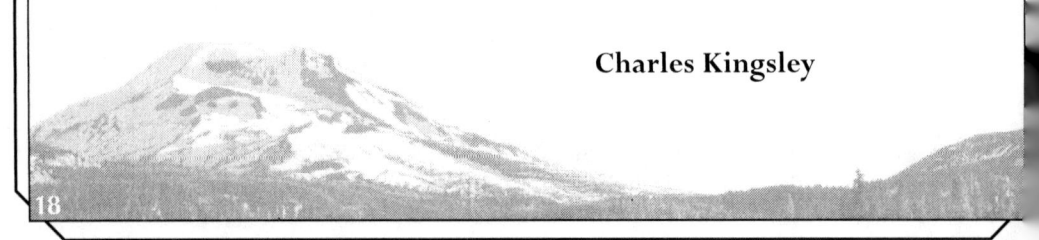

Charles Kingsley

Living a Life of Purpose

It doesn't matter if you try and try and try again, and fail. It does matter if you try and fail, and fail to try again.

Charles F. Kettering

Living a Life of Purpose

Success is getting up just one more time than you fall down.

Anonymous

Living a Life of Purpose

If you think you're too small to have an impact, try going to bed with a mosquito.

Anita Roddick

Living a Life of Purpose

To keep a lamp burning we have to keep putting oil in it.

Mother Teresa

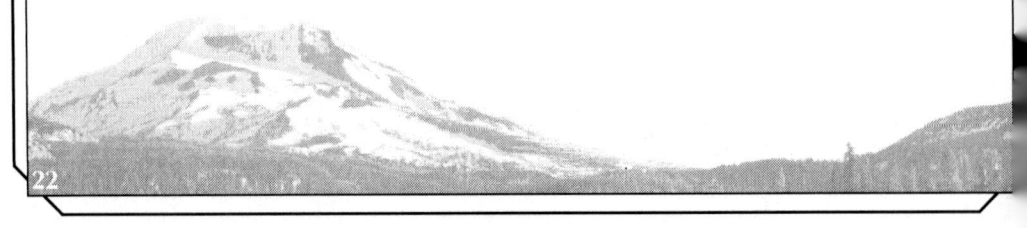

Living a Life of Purpose

How far you go in life depends on your being tender with the young, compassionate with the aged, sympathetic with the striving and tolerant of the weak and the strong.

George Washington Carver

Living a Life of Purpose

Each failure serves as a rung in the ladder of success.

Edward A. Gloeggler

Living a Life of Purpose

What volunteers bring is the human touch, the individual, caring approach that no government program, however well-meaning and well-executed, can deliver.

Edward James Olmos

Living a Life of Purpose

There are some people who live in a dream world, and there are some who face reality, and then there are those who turn one into the other.

Douglas Everett

Living a Life of Purpose

Occasionally in life there are those moments of unutterable fulfillment which cannot be completely explained by those symbols called words. Their meanings can only be articulated by the inaudible language of the heart.

Martin Luther King, Jr.

Living a Life of Purpose

In all giving, give thought. With thoughtful giving, even small sums may accomplish great purposes.

Fred G. Meyer

Living a Life of Purpose

Cautious, careful people, always casting about to preserve their reputation and social standing, never can bring about a reform.

Susan B. Anthony

Living a Life of Purpose

The secrets of success do not work unless you do.

John A. Hamilton, Jr.

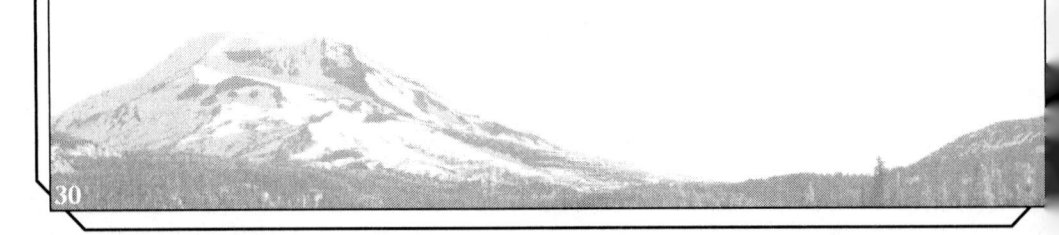

Living a Life of Purpose

The key to realizing a dream is to focus not on success but significance – and then even the small steps and little victories along your path will take on greater meaning.

Oprah Winfrey

Living a Life of Purpose

The rewards go to the risk-takers, those who are willing to put their egos on the line and reach out to other people and to a richer fuller life for themselves.

Susan Roane

Living a Life of Purpose

There's no substitute for guts.

Paul "Bear" Bryant

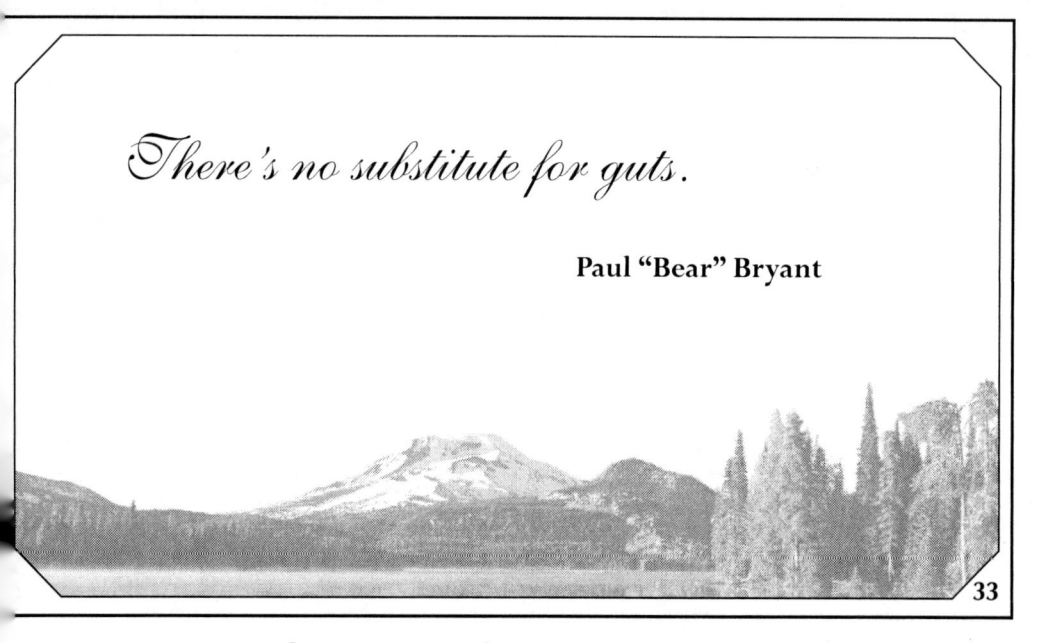

Living a Life of Purpose

Three words take on their true meaning when we see them as verbs more than nouns: volunteer, love, God.

Sue Vineyard

Living a Life of Purpose

That's what I consider true generosity. You give your all and yet you always feel as if it costs you nothing.

Simone de Beauvoir

Living a Life of Purpose

And we know that all things work together for good to them that love God, to them who are the called according to His purpose.

Romans 8:28 KJV

Living a Life of Purpose

A life devoid of service to others is a life devoid of meaning.

Marianne Williamson

Living a Life of Purpose

What you do as a volunteer is much more meaningful than what you do for a paycheck.

Frances Clapp

Living a Life of Purpose

Set goals in life; set them high and persist until they are achieved. Once they are achieved, set bigger and better goals. You will soon find that your life will become happier and more purposeful by working toward positive goals.

Raymond Floyd

Living a Life of Purpose

There are three ways to get something done: Do it yourself, employ someone, or forbid your children to do it.

Montana Crane

Living a Life of Purpose

Keep on beginning and failing. Each time you fail, start all over gain, and you will grow stronger until you have accomplished a purpose – not the one you began with perhaps, but one you'll be glad to remember.

Anne Sullivan

Living a Life of Purpose

Anyone who has never made a mistake has never tried anything new.

Albert Einstein

Living a Life of Purpose

Do one thing at a time and do that one thing as if your life depended on it.

Eugene Grace

Living a Life of Purpose

The man or woman without a purpose is like a ship without a rudder. Have a purpose in life and throw the strength of mind and muscle into your work that God has given you.

Thomas Carlyle

Living a Life of Purpose

A ship in harbor is safe – but that is not what ships are for.

Unknown

Living a Life of Purpose

Never doubt that a small group of thoughtful, committed citizens can change the world; indeed, it's the only thing that ever has.

Margaret Mead

Living a Life of Purpose

Service is the rent we pay for living. It is the very purpose of life, not something you do in your spare time.

Marian Wright Edelman

Living a Life of Purpose

To find in ourselves what makes life worth living is risky business, for it means that once we know we must seek it. It also means that without it life will be valueless.

Marsha Sinetar

Living a Life of Purpose

The sole meaning of life is to serve humanity.

Leo Tolstoy

Living a Life of Purpose

What one loves in childhood stays in the heart forever.

Mary Jo Putney

Living a Life of Purpose

Standing in the middle of the road is very dangerous; you get knocked down by the traffic from both sides.

Margaret Thatcher

Living a Life of Purpose

I am convinced that the difference between the weak and the powerful, the great and the insignificant is energy, invincible determination and purpose.

Powell Buxton

Living a Life of Purpose

I am always more interested in what I am about to do than in what I have already done.

Rachel Carson

Living a Life of Purpose

When people are serving, life is no longer meaningless.

John W. Gardner

Living a Life of Purpose

What really matters is what you do with what you have.

Shirley Lord

Living a Life of Purpose

I totally reject the view that the only business of business is business. The purpose of business is to serve society.

Kenneth N. Dayton

Living a Life of Purpose

Act boldly and unseen forces will come to your aid.

Dorothea Brande

Living a Life of Purpose

Nobody really cares if you're miserable, so you might as well be happy.

Cynthia Nelms

Living a Life of Purpose

Work is either fun or drudgery. It depends on your attitude. I like fun.

Colleen C. Barrett

Living a Life of Purpose

The smallest deed is better than the grandest intention.

Anonymous

Living a Life of Purpose

Faith sees the invisible, believes the unbelievable, and receives the impossible.

Corrie Ten Boom

Living a Life of Purpose

No one is ever completely useless: you can always serve as a horrible example.

American Proverb

Living a Life of Purpose

Be not simply good; be good for something.

Henry David Thoreau

Living a Life of Purpose

Power is the ability to do good things for others.

Brooke Astor

Living a Life of Purpose

Want to live it up? Then live up to your potential.

Sheree Parris Nudd

Living a Life of Purpose

To live a creative life, we must lose our fear of being wrong.

Joseph Chilton Pearce

Living a Life of Purpose

Have courage for the greatest sorrows of life and patience for the small ones, and when you have laboriously accomplished your daily tasks, go to sleep in peace. God is awake.

Victor Hugo

Living a Life of Purpose

The central purpose of each life should be to dilute the misery in the world.

Karl Menninger

Living a Life of Purpose

The rich are only trustees of the money they possess. Wealth should be used for purposeful benevolence. Those who wait to give it away until they're dead, show that they would not give it if they could keep it longer.

Joseph Hall

Living a Life of Purpose

Success is not measured by how you do compared to how somebody else does. Success is measured by how you do compared to what you could have done with what God gave you.

Anonymous

Living a Life of Purpose

Turning it over in your mind won't plow the field.

Irish Proverb

Living a Life of Purpose

You can't build a reputation on what you're going to do.

Henry Ford

Living a Life of Purpose

Doing is a quantum leap from imagining. Thinking about swimming isn't much like actually getting in the water.

Barbara Sher

Living a Life of Purpose

It is better to begin in the evening than not at all.

English Proverb

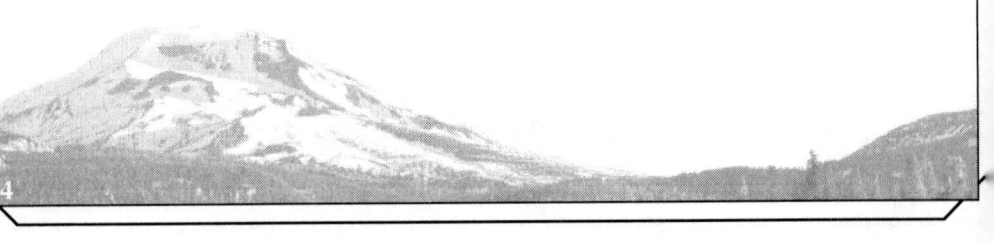

Living a Life of Purpose

If we did all the things we are capable of doing, we would truly astound ourselves.

Thomas Edison

Living a Life of Purpose

It is great to have friends when one is young, and more so when you are getting old. When we are young, friends are taken for granted. In old age we know how meaningful they are.

Edvard Grieg

Living a Life of Purpose

Remember not only to say the right thing in the right place, but far more difficult still, to leave unsaid the wrong thing at the tempting moment.

Benjamin Franklin

Living a Life of Purpose

Deciding who to give money to, how much to give and for what purpose, is neither an easy matter or in every man's power. Such excellence is rare, praiseworthy, and noble.

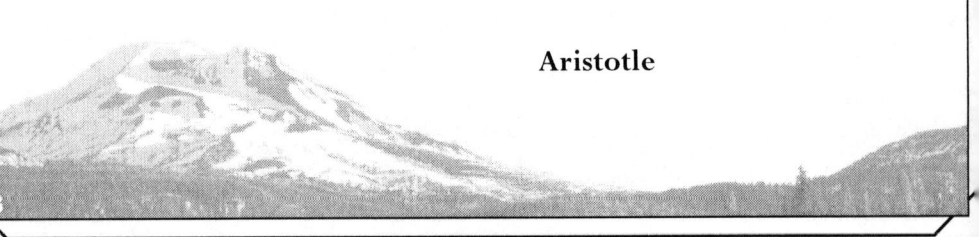

Aristotle

Living a Life of Purpose

A man has made at least a start on discovering the meaning of human life when he plants shade trees under which he knows full well he will never sit.

Elton Trueblood

Living a Life of Purpose

Let us be of good cheer, remembering that the misfortunes hardest to bear are those which never come.

Amy Lowell

Living a Life of Purpose

Adversity reveals genius, prosperity conceals it.

Horace

Living a Life of Purpose

One can never consent to creep when one feels an impulse to soar.

Helen Keller

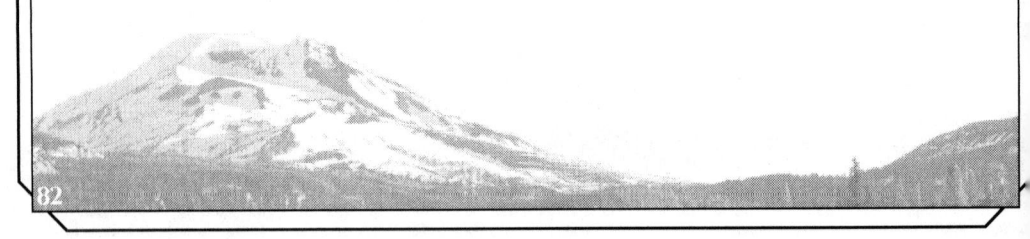

Living a Life of Purpose

To be nobody but yourself – in a world which is doing its best, night and day, to make you like everybody else – means to fight the hardest battle which any human being can fight, and never stop fighting.

e.e. cummings

Living a Life of Purpose

No matter what age you are, or what your circumstances might be, you are special, and you still have something to offer. Your life, because of who you are, has meaning.

Barbara De Angelis

Living a Life of Purpose

Every action we take, everything we do, is either a victory or defeat in the struggle to become what we want to be.

Anne Byrhhe

Living a Life of Purpose

Every great oak tree was once a nut that stood its ground.

Anonymous

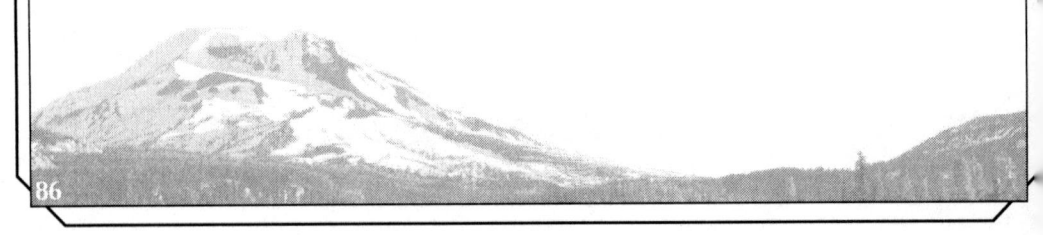

Living a Life of Purpose

The results of philanthropy are always beyond calculation.

Miriam Beard

Living a Life of Purpose

Give life meaning through your commitments.

Paul Reinert

Living a Life of Purpose

> *I am definitely going to take a course on time management . . . just as soon as I can work it into my schedule.*
>
> **Louis E. Boone**

Living a Life of Purpose

The greater danger for most of us is not that our aim is too high and we miss it, but that it is too low and we reach it.

Michelangelo

Living a Life of Purpose

Learn to laugh at your troubles and you'll never run out of things to laugh at.

Lyn Karol

Living a Life of Purpose

We can't take any credit for our talents. It's how we use them that counts.

Madeleine L'Engle

Living a Life of Purpose

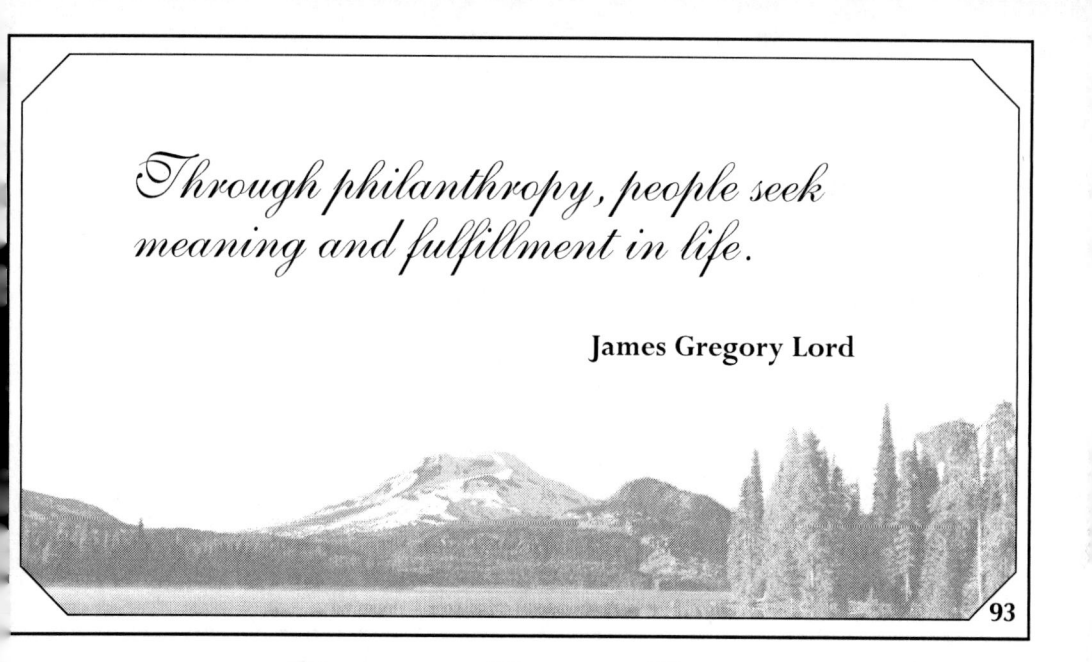

> *Through philanthropy, people seek meaning and fulfillment in life.*
>
> **James Gregory Lord**

Living a Life of Purpose

The ultimate test of man's conscience may be his willingness to sacrifice something today for future generations whose words of thanks will not be heard.

Gaylord Nelson

Living a Life of Purpose

There is only one happiness in life, to love and be loved.

George Sand

Living a Life of Purpose

You can have what it is you want, or you can have your reasons for not having it.

Werner Erhard

Living a Life of Purpose

Don't be afraid to take a big step if one is indicated. You can't cross a chasm in two small jumps.

David Lloyd George

Living a Life of Purpose

The moment one definitely commits oneself, then Providence moves, too. All sorts of things occur to help one that would never have otherwise occurred.

Johann Wolfgang Von Goethe

Living a Life of Purpose

I resolved to take Fate by the throat and shake the living out of her.

Louisa May Alcott

Living a Life of Purpose

Though no one can go back and make a brand new start, anyone can start from now and make a brand new ending.

Carl Bard

Living a Life of Purpose

Go confidently in the direction of your dreams! Live the life you've imagined.

Henry David Thoreau

Living a Life of Purpose

This is another in the *"Living"* series of gift books.

The *"Living"* books are available in bulk quantities. Schools, hospitals, other nonprofit organizations or businesses can also order personalized covers incorporating the organization's name to pass along to friends.

To see our complete line, visit www.DesignsforGiving.com

La Tour Press   P.O. Box 506   Brookeville, MD 20833

Living a Life of Purpose